FULHAM PHOTOS

VOLUME TWO

FULHAM PHOTOS
VOLUME TWO

MORE MOMENTS AND MEMORIES

Words and pictures by
KEN COTON

ASHWATER
PRESS

FULHAM PHOTOS
VOLUME TWO

First published in October 2014

Copyright © Ken Coton 2014

The right of Ken Coton to be identified as the author
of all material in this book has been asserted by him
in accordance with the Copyright, Designs and Patent Act 1988.

All photographs are copyright © Ken Coton.

Designed and published by
Ashwater Press
68 Tranmere Road
Whitton, Twickenham, Middlesex, TW2 7JB

Printed and bound by Henry Ling Limited, Dorchester, England

ISBN 978-0-9927119-1-7

Foreword

by Les Strong

WHEN KEN asked me if I'd do the foreword for his new book, I thought it was yet another of his endless jokes (yes, believe it or not, he's funny). On finding out he was serious, I said yes immediately before he changed his mind.

It is of course an honour and a privilege to be able to contribute to this book and to a man who is so synonymous with Fulham over the decades. Ken logged my whole career at Fulham with his camera, yet when I ask him if he can dig out an action picture of me he usually says he'll try but can't guarantee he has any (I think he's joking).

I have every one of Ken's books, both solo or in collaboration, and they are an endless source of pleasure.

Without Ken's pictures there would virtually be no pictorial history of our great club. He has tens of thousands of pictures – many that have never been published, and some you'll be seeing for the first time in this book.

The word 'legend' gets bandied about a little too easily for my liking nowadays, but without a doubt Ken Coton is a true Fulham legend. He has taken many magnificent pictures that have charted the ups and downs of our wonderful club, many capturing the endless fun to be had at Fulham over the decades.

I'm proud to say Ken is a friend of mine and I was delighted when he agreed to take the photographs at my wedding, although asking my wife Laura to dive full length in her wedding dress was a bit much.

This book will sit proudly alongside all the others and I know will be read over and over again. I'm certain that you too will enjoy this book and take pleasure in the knowledge that every one of the pictures you will see was taken with the love of Fulham at its core.

But there is no time to rest on your laurels, Ken. Keep looking and one day you may finally find that action picture of yours truly.

Special thanks to colleague Robert Fennell for his editorial advice throughout the book. Against his better judgement he even allowed me the word 'selfie'. Although it was a recent word of the year – and was approved by Susie Dent of Countdown's Dictionary Corner – he wishes to disassociate himself from it. In spite of that, his support is much appreciated.

Introduction

More Moments and Memories

WELCOME TO a further selection of pictures from my archive of Fulham photographs. It was twelve years ago that I produced the first volume of pictures, and I didn't want to rush into a second book. For one thing, I wasn't sure that I had enough interesting photographs to fill a second volume, but I finally decided to dig deep into my boxes of pictures, and I hope you feel this current venture is worthwhile. This collection of pictures is a mix of a few old favourites (indulge me, please!), some photos that have appeared previously only once (often many years ago), together with a whole lot that have never before seen the light of day.

I have been spurred on by colleague Martin Plumb, and I thank him for that. He is so good with details and Fulham facts that I have dubbed him the Statmaster, and I asked him to supply observations throughout the book. Where Martin has added extra information, his words appear separately below mine, thus distinguishing his facts from my ramblings.

I look back fondly on my years at Fulham and I'm greatly proud and thankful for the opportunity I had to chronicle our great club. At the time of writing I have renewed my season ticket for a great view of the Championship from the Johnny Haynes stand. Let's hope the season brings more joy to us supporters than did the last season!

It's over fifty years since I took my first Fulham pictures – so I must be getting on a bit. In the normal scheme of things, therefore, you may be spared a third volume of *Fulham Photos*. In the meantime I do hope you enjoy this collection of pictures, many of which I had truly forgotten I had taken!

Which club has had three managers who have also managed England? It's Fulham, of course (Bobby Robson, Kevin Keegan and Roy Hodgson), and it's the sort of thing that makes us feel a real warmth towards our club. I trust that the pictures in this book give some indication of the genuine friendliness and affection that I felt during my time at Craven Cottage. That would be a great achievement for this book.

One regret is that many of Fulham's fine players from recent years do not appear in this book – players like Brian McBride and Danny Murphy – as I didn't cover their matches. I would certainly have relished some sort of 'roving' status to continue capturing the passing scene at the Cottage. Even though that eluded me, it is an idea that the club could consider – television footage doesn't produce good books!

My thanks to international football manager Les Strong for his foreword to the book (yes, he was the coach of Anguilla). It is purely coincidental, but he does seem to creep into many of the pictures. Les typifies the spirit of real Fulham – approachable, professional, yet full of fun. To preserve his reputation (I do believe he has one), I must point out that Les has had no association with any of the captions in the book!

It's usual for supporters' words to end with 'COYW'.

So, with much affection I say: 'Come on, you Whites!"

Ken Coton
Whitton, September 2014

So, the first picture in the book features Chelsea. Well, it had to be someone! This looks like a good shout for a penalty, but I'm sure we didn't get it.

* * *

The Statmaster writes: It's February 1966 and the Whites are mired in their annual relegation struggle. The Fulham player being tackled by Chelsea's Marvin Hinton is winger Terry Parmenter, who was vying for a wing position with the young Les Barrett. Parmenter was a volatile player who never really established himself in the team over five years at the Cottage. The other Fulham player is Mark (Pancho) Pearson, who had been part of the post-Munich Manchester United team. In the background on the left is future England manager Terry Venables, shadowed by Fulham's Fred Callaghan. They were old friends, but were both sent off for fisticuffs the following season at White Hart Lane after Venables joined Spurs.

I clearly remember taking some jolly pictures of our 'Three Musketeers', when Jimmy Conway, Steve Earle and Les Barrett posed with corner flags. However, this looks like the end of the photography session, as the trio seem to be suggesting politely that my time is up.

On a mudheap of a pitch our George Best still manages to display his skills; this was at Wolves in February 1977. George always gave his best for us.

*   *   *

Best is here tackled by Scottish international midfielder Willie Carr, formerly of Coventry. Fulham lost this match 1–5, and at the time were rock bottom and in the middle of a thirteen-match winless streak. However, the Cottagers managed to escape relegation – and Wolves ended up as league champions.

This is one of my earliest action pictures, taken on the opening day of the 1962–63 season, and shows the sublime Graham Leggat scoring one of his two goals in the 2–1 victory that day over Leicester City. Goalkeeper Gordon Banks is well beaten; actually we seemed to beat Leicester often and easily in those days!

Graham is a bit of a blur in the photo, mainly because the picture was taken on a very simple camera (pictured here). It made me realise that I needed a more sophisticated camera with faster shutter speeds – though I reckon it would have needed a shutter speed of just a 1/1000th of a second to freeze the flying Leggat!

*   *   *   *

Also in the picture is another of Fulham's Scottish internationals, Jackie Henderson, rarely glimpsed in Ken's photographs. Although past his best when he signed from Arsenal, he proved a useful acquisition and had helped Fulham avoid relegation the previous season, whilst reaching the FA Cup semi-final. Later in the 1962–63 season he sadly broke his leg in a league match at Blackburn, which effectively ended his career.

During the early 1970s a stand was built on the riverside terraces. It was officially opened in February 1972, celebrated with a visit from the Portuguese champions, Benfica. The Benfica star was Eusebio, and I just had to try to get a good picture of him in action (meaning I was at the wrong end to capture any Fulham goals...). It was a freezing evening, but I managed to click at just the right moment as Eusebio scored with a shot from the edge of the penalty area. I hardly had time to focus as well, and I fear John Richardson and Reg Matthewson are a bit sharper in the picture than the great man. Nevertheless, I got the goal! Oh, and Fulham won the match 3–2.

*   *   *

Not only was this a cold evening, but there were power cuts and the ground was powered by generators. Benfica had been Portuguese champions nine times in the previous twelve years, and in the World Cup year of 1966 had provided several of the superb Portugal side that were (unluckily) beaten by England in the semi-final.

In the Fulham match Benfica were two goals down within twenty minutes thanks to a strike from Steve Earle and a glancing header from Roger Cross. Benfica pulled a goal back just before half-time through Diamantino. Fulham's new keeper Peter Mellor excelled throughout the match with fine saves, notably from Jordao and Diamantino. With twenty minutes left, Cross scored his second of the night with the aid of a deflection, before Eusebio's late thunderbolt, captured by Ken.

Eusebio was one of several players recruited from Portugal's African colonies, and in 1968 had topped Benfica's scoring chart with forty-two goals in just twenty-six matches. With blistering pace and ferocious shooting he was the star of the 1966 World Cup. Eusebio da Silva Ferreira, a true gentleman and a great ambassador for football, passed away early in 2014, aged seventy-one.

Here are some of the pictures I took at the post-match reception in the Riverside suite. At top, England manager Alf Ramsey gets advice from Fulham coach Ken Craggs (at right in picture), while Fulham's World Cup hero George Cohen looks on. Above left are 'Big Match' stars Brian Moore and Jimmy Hill. The other picture is of perhaps the most illustrious dignitary present that evening – my dear Dad.

*   *   *

Also present were the Portuguese ambassador; the president of FIFA, Sir Stanley Rous; and the president of the Football League, Len Shipman. Others attending included QPR manager (and former Fulham coach) Gordon Jago, Millwall manager Benny Fenton, and Tommy Docherty.

Ouch! A defender sends winger John Evanson crashing on to the cinder track, courtesy of a Seventies-type tackle. No need for today's 'I felt contact, so I went down...'

The linesman (Do I have to call him an assistant referee? For heaven's sake, he's a linesman) sports a full Seventies beard and tache, and the defender flaunts a full head of Seventies hair.

I found this print at the bottom of a box of pictures and can't remember when it was taken, or who the opponents were. The Statmaster thinks it could be Oxford United or Millwall.

Left: 'A Foggy Day in London Town...'

In the picture above, it looks like it's Graham Leggat who's celebrating Johnny Haynes' goal in the 2–2 draw against Manchester United in March 1964. Leggat has already turned to join his team-mates, yet the goalkeeper is still in mid air, and the position of the ball looks distinctly unreal.

Could it be that the picture has been tampered with? Was the ball put in the photograph with scissors and paste? (No computer manipulation in those days.)

Well, no. I've never done that sort of thing, and nor has Ashwater, of course. However, look at the picture on the right. The picture is an interloper, as I didn't take it. It's a press photo of our Jim Langley in action at Molineux. I've put it in because of what's written on the back of the original: 'Artist, please move ball down to here.' Yes, the ball had been cut out and pasted in a more favourable position.

*   *   *

Langley was formerly with Leeds United and Brighton, and was originally a left winger before converting to full back. When he played for England with Haynes in 1960 it was the last time that an England team contained two Fulham players.

Langley was renowned for his sporting and gentlemanly behaviour, his crew-cut hair, his bandy legs, his immaculate sliding tackles, his long throw-ins – and his acrobatic bicycle-kick clearances, as demonstrated here.

I was much saddened to learn of the death of Dennis Turner in January 2014. It was Dennis who twenty years ago cajoled me to produce *Fulham's Golden Years*, the first Ashwater book about Fulham. We subsequently co-operated on many books. He was a hard taskmaster, but he knew his stuff and was a true Fulham fan who became a director of the club.

Applause in tribute to him before the match against Southampton on February 1st (above) was touching and deserved. A genuine Fulham legend – but he never played for the club! How he would have liked to be part of the players' statistics he so assiduously compiled.

In 2002 we won a cup! OK, it was the Intertoto Cup, but we won. In the final we beat Bologna 5–3 over two legs. This picture comes from the second leg, played at our then home ground of Loftus Road. What a great moment as fans and players celebrate a goal from Junichi Inamoto, one of three he scored that evening in the 3–1 win. The Fulham players are, from front, Facundo Sava, Steve Marlet and Sylvain Legwinski.

I needed the Statmaster to identify the Fulham player pictured here flying down the wing. I didn't recall who it was, but at least I was happy that the player was sharp in the picture.

*   *   *

The picture shows the young Fabrice Fernandes outpacing two Barnsley players including stalwart Chris Morgan (left). Fabrice was part of Jean Tigana's promotion-winning team of 2000–01. Barnsley were beaten 5–1 in the heat and had a player sent off more in desperation than malice. It was the day that Louis Saha fully announced himself on the Fulham stage with a sparkling first-half hat-trick. Whilst acknowledging Fulham's class, Barnsley manager Dave Bassett conceded that Fulham hadn't been given a great test, saying, 'They had time to put the deckchairs out and smoke the cigars.'

Fernandes remained an enigma. With obvious talent and typical Gallic swagger, he looked a star of the future, but was sometimes a law unto himself and seemed not to have an appetite for the physical side of the game. He didn't last long in the rigours of the Premiership and his career in Britain fizzled out after spells with Glasgow Rangers and Southampton.

The lovely Ted Drake poses for my camera with the equally lovely Yvonne Haines on a sunny day in the late 1970s. Ted was working with the Fulham youth players and Yvonne was club secretary. Ted once scored seven goals for Arsenal in a match at Aston Villa, a feat not matched by Yvonne.

Younger fans may not be aware that for two years we had a Fulham rugby league team playing regularly at the Cottage. The team provided a lot of excitement and passion, and attracted large attendances. The team has since gone through a number of name and venue changes, and at the time of writing is called the London Broncos, based at The Hive in Edgware.

This is a try from the last match of the inaugural season, against Doncaster in April 1981. I wasn't sure of the identity of the try scorer, though I know that it's captain Reg Bowden on the ground watching the action. So it was over to Peter Lush of London League Publications, a renowned rugby league buff, to get more details. Thank you, Peter; it can be confirmed that the scorer is David Eckersley, and Fulham won the match 37–11, their biggest score of the season. At the end of the season, Fulham Rugby League were promoted from Division Two to the top tier.

The Statmaster thinks that the try-scorer looks remarkably like Ray Houghton and the opposition player directly behind his head looks remarkably like former Manchester City player Mike Summerbee! In the circumstances he was happy to defer to Mr Lush.

All eyes on the ball at Exeter in September 1980, as Tony Mahoney is 'persuaded' not to get involved in a possible goal opportunity. I regret I can't remember the actual incident, but from the shadows on the pitch it looks as though the ball is heading for goal. However, the next picture I took (right) shows the keeper smothering the ball, suggesting that the ball hit the post and rebounded back. Gordon Davies looks on from on high.

This was a costly miss, as we lost the match 0–1.

Rarely did I cover our defence, as I wanted to capture Fulham goals, but I did so in October 1978 during our match against Preston. The fact that Les Strong kindly provided a foreword for this book in no way influenced my choice of this picture, but it does show Les in sparkling form (his words, not mine) thwarting a Preston attack. In Les's shadow is Tony Gale, and in the background are Terry Bullivant and Ray Evans.

* * *

Preston played in a yellow away strip to avoid clashing with Fulham's white shirts. This was a very entertaining encounter on an unseasonably warm afternoon which Fulham won 5–3 with five different scorers on the mark – a rare event in itself. (Of course Ken was at the wrong end to chronicle that feat...) Amongst the goalscorers was Kevin Lock, a summer signing from West Ham, with his first goal for the club. Kevin was part of the West Ham team that had beaten us in the 1975 FA Cup final.

The Preston forward is Michael Robinson, just starting out on his career. At the end of the season, Malcolm Allison at Manchester City paid out £750,000 for him, an enormous fee for a young player with no top-flight experience. The gamble failed and Robinson moved on to Brighton where he rebuilt his reputation. He finished his career in Spain, where he now has a respected sports media role.

The Statmaster himself stars in this picture, together with our very own David Hamilton – two Ashwater authors, watched over by another Fulham legend, the superb Brian McBride.

It's not often that David is lost for words, but it looks as though Martin is in full flight, possibly telling David the precise number of substitutions he has announced over his Fulham match hosting career. David's warm and reassuring tone has seen our club through many ups and downs over the years.

In 2002, after one year in the Premiership, we had to vacate Craven Cottage so that it could be upgraded and made all-seater. And so we found ourselves at our new home ground, QPR's Loftus Road – and my picture is from the very first match there, against Bolton Wanderers on August 17th. It was a warm sunny day, we won 4–1 and all seemed well with the world. There was, nevertheless, a nagging doubt as to whether we would ever return to the Cottage, but thankfully we did, just two years later.

The Fulham dancers, the Cravenettes, featured in the first Fulham Photos book, and they duly welcomed the players on this occasion, but, of course, their appearance in this picture in no way influenced my decision to include it here.

This was a recent reunion of some members of our FA Cup campaign of 1975. What a treat it was for me to meet them again. One or two of them even knew who I was.

Here's the line-up on the edge of the famous Craven Cottage turf: from left. Ken Craggs (coach), Les Strong, John Collins (coach), John Fraser, John Mitchell, Barry Lloyd, Les Barrett and John Lacy.

Manager Jean Tigana holds the trophy, and chairman Mohamed Al Fayed holds the scarf that tells it all. The picture was taken during the celebrations at the end of our final home match that season, a season during which we accumulated over 100 points.

*   *   *

Although all seems rosy here and Mr Al Fayed looks happy at the prospect of competing in the Premiership, relations between the pair would become strained within eighteen months in the light of Tigana's transfer deals. Within two years, Tigana and his coaching team of Damiano and Propos had all left the club.

Watched by Barry Lloyd, our centre forward Viv Busby bursts into the penalty area, deceiving defenders. This was against Charlton in November 1975. No goal for Busby on this occasion, but Lloyd got our goal in the 1–1 draw. In the background is Tyrone James who made just a few appearances during his four-year stint at the club.

*   *   *

At left in the picture is Charlton stalwart Keith Peacock, the first player ever to take the field as a substitute in the Football League. That was in August 1965. Peacock was a great one-club man, making more than 600 appearances for the Addicks over eighteen years.

A flying header from Wayne Collins in the 2–0 victory over Wycombe Wanderers in September 1998 providing a pleasing picture for my camera. The goals that evening were scored by Paul Bracewell and Chris Coleman, who later became our manager. Coleman missed only one match during the whole of that championship-winning season.

* * *

Bracewell's goal that evening was his only one for the club. Paul became our manager the following season.

Gus Uhlenbeek fires in a centre against Leigh RMI in the FA Cup in November 1998.

*   *   *

This third-round tie against non-league opposition was memorable for a Dirk Lehmann headed goal and many inspired saves from the Leigh goalkeeper David Felgate that earned the minnows a 1–1 draw. Fortunately the Whites negotiated a difficult replay 2–0.

Steve Finnan fires in a centre against Chesterfield in the league in November 1998.

*   *   *

This was Steve's debut for the Cottagers following his £600,000 move from Notts County. A Paul Peschisolido brace secured a 2–1 victory that day over the Spireites. Finnan was an inspired signing by manager Keegan and made over 200 appearances for Fulham before moving to Liverpool in 2003.

We rarely get much joy from Arsenal. In all our history we never beat them at Highbury, and only occasionally won against them at the Cottage. This was not one of those times. Our third ever home match in the Premiership was a visit from the Gunners in September 2001, and we ended up on the wrong end of a 1–3 scoreline. I managed to capture our goal from the terraces (yes, it was still terraces then), which saw Steed Malbranque scoring from close range past David Seaman. The other Arsenal players are, from left, Martin Keown, Patrick Vieira, Sol Campbell and Lauren.

*   *   *

This was Malbranque's first goal for the club; he went on to score 40 more over five seasons – a tidy return for a midfield player.

No need to point out that this was a rather muddy pitch. Yet it hosted a crucial Second Division relegation dogfight, as Fulham travelled to Cardiff in March 1972. The Cottagers lost the match 0–1, though the picture suggests that Roger Cross's close-range header is destined for the bottom corner of the Cardiff goal to give the visitors an equaliser. In fact, the goalkeeper made a truly world-class save.

*   *   *

The tractor marks beside the goal hint at how difficult it had been to get the match played at all. Although Fulham lost the match, they just managed to escape relegation on the final day of the season, though by just one point, as did Cardiff. Next to Cross in the picture is Cardiff skipper Don Murray, and in front of the referee is the Bluebirds' ex-Coventry international Ian Gibson.

John Mitchell has just given Fulham the lead early in the second half of the FA Cup semi-final against Birmingham in 1975, and he rushes to the massed Fulham faithful to celebrate his twenty-yard wonder strike.

*   *   *

Fulham had dominated their first-division opponents before this goal, but lost a little concentration after that and allowed Birmingham a scrappy and undeserved equaliser to force a draw. However, it all came right on the night in the last minute of extra time in the replay at Maine Road a few days later, as another John Mitchell goal took Fulham to Wembley.

I can still hear the sound of this goal, an Allan Clarke equaliser in the 2–2 draw at Anfield in October 1966. The sound wasn't a roar or even a cheer, just the swish of the ball hitting the netting at the back of the goal – followed by an eerie silence from the unbelieving Scousers. By contrast, I was jumping inside with delight!

*   *   *   **

Reds defenders Geoff Strong (10) and Chris Lawler complain to the referee for a perceived foul on goalkeeper Tommy Lawrence (bottom right in the picture), but he is having none of it. Goalscorer Clarke was in the middle of a purple patch after scoring four goals for the England U-23 side in his first international match. Between October and the New Year he netted fifteen goals in all domestic competitions.

A night match at a gloomy Leicester City in March 1979. Gloomy was the light and gloomy was the result, as we lost 0–1. Flying down the wing, trying to get the attack going, is elegant midfielder John Beck, with socks rolled down. The Fulham player at left is a mustachioed Les Strong, and in the background is Richard Money.

*   *   *

Beck had been signed from Coventry City for a substantial £80,000 fee after starting his career at QPR. But he was part of a poor Fulham team in decline (not including you, Les, of course) and Cottage fans never truly saw the best of him. He moved on to Bournemouth early in Malcolm Macdonald's time as manager. After his career of over 500 games was finished early by injury, Beck did have managerial success, particularly at Cambridge United.

Wow! Fulham's record signing, Peter Kitchen, crashes home a goal against the mighty Arsenal. But wait a minute, this was in September 1979, and Arsenal hadn't visited the Cottage for many years. It had to be a special occasion – and of course it was. It was a testimonial match for Ted Drake (see page 20), who at that time was working as part of manager Malcolm Macdonald's back-room team, and was a director and life president of the club.

Bought for a record fee of £150,000, star forward Kitchen failed to achieve at Fulham, partly due to injuries, and scored just six goals in twenty-four appearances. The other Fulham player in the picture is Chris Guthrie.

* * *

Kitchen's shot is watched by former Chelsea star John Hollins, and the other two Arsenal defenders are Willie Young and Pat Rice. Ted Drake had two spells with Fulham, initially assisting manager Vic Buckingham during the mid-Sixties for a couple of years. He was very briefly Fulham's acting manager following the sacking of Bobby Campbell in October 1980. Drake's son, Bobby, played sporadically as a full back for Fulham during the Sixties. A genial and popular man, Drake died in 1995 aged 82.

It's half-time on a sunny afternoon in the mid-Sixties. The flags are flying in the breeze, there's the programme to be read, and half-time scores are awaited on the newfangled electronic scoreboard.

* * *

The haircuts on view – short back and sides, a Tony Curtis or a Boston and 'something for the weekend' – are typical of the era, whilst a classic Dad, complete with Harold Wilson pipe, is still permitted to ruminate on the first half with a few puffs inside the ground.

Opposite: Allan Clarke coolly slots home a goal at Newcastle in October 1967. In the excitement of Fulham scoring a goal, I always tried to keep my cool as well and immediately take a picture of the ball in the net, and the one I took on this occasion adds colour to the moment. Young fans sit round the edge of the pitch, whilst a photographer has stopped taking pictures with his Rolleiflex, a strange camera where you viewed the scene by looking down into the top. I note he's sitting on the ground; I found out long ago that it's not easy to get out of the way of an onrushing player from that position!

* * *

Fulham are playing in their all-blue away strip, and Les Barrett (in the background) has just passed to the unmarked Clarke, beating the offside trap. Clarke easily beats the former Hearts keeper Gordon Marshall. After the goal, Fulham dominated the game but, as was pretty symptomatic of that relegation season, lost to two late, controversial goals.

I had to be sharp to get this goal, as it was scored in the very first minute. No leisurely fiddling with camera settings, it was 'Camera, action'! The action was from George Best who flashed in a headed goal past a startled keeper in the League Cup tie against Bolton in October 1976.

*   *   *

The goalkeeper is Barry Siddall. Bolton claw the game back to 2–2 to earn a replay at Burnden Park. And what a replay it was! With Fulham leading 2–1 the unpredictable referee Kevin McNally adds on eight minutes at the end of the match, during which time Bolton scramble an equaliser. The team protest about the amount of time added on, and McNally makes a name for himself by sending off Fulham's Bobby Moore for dissent. (Note from Ken: See page 24 of the first Fulham Photos.) This prompts a furious walk-off by the entire Fulham team, led by manager Alec Stock. After a tense stand-off lasting several minutes, the team finally emerges following an ultimatum from the embattled official. In a muted period of extra time, no further goals are scored. So Fulham – no strangers now to cup marathons – play a third tie at St Andrews, but bow out 1–2, seemingly rather disinterested in the match, no doubt feeling somewhat aggrieved by the events of the previous game.

And here's our second goal from the League Cup tie featured opposite. It's all eyes on John Mitchell as he scores from five yards, with Rodney Marsh in close attendance. I must admit it looks suspiciously like offside, unless there were Bolton players not in the camera's view!

*   *   *

Is Mitchell active, or passive or neutral; is this first phase or second phase; was Mitch interfering with play? If you thought offside was difficult years ago, it's almost incomprehensible now. FIFA have a lot to answer for.

This picture appeared in the Fulham programme for the match against West Brom in August 1975. Yes, it is a cup we won, and here it's being presented by manager Alec Stock. The recipients are Fulham's quiz team and they had just won the coveted Southern Counties Supporters Quiz Cup by a 93–90 scoreline over Gravesend FC. Team captain Colin Kempster is at left, and other team members are (from left) Vic Read, John Disspain, Keith Evemy, Mike Ryley and Adrian Knowles. Our Statmaster is intrigued by the admiring glances of the two heavy rock musicians on the left. He also points out that Colin was Fulham's first real DJ and match announcer, and his warm tones punctuated many a miserable afternoon.

Opposite: It's that man Clarke again, this time poaching a goal at Coventry in November 1967, and I couldn't help adding an aftermath picture as Clarke raises his arm in trademark salute. No raucous over-the-top celebration for Clarke, no mass hug for the Fulham team. Probably just a brisk, manly handshake.

* * *

This was five minutes from the end of the match – and at the end of a glorious five-man Fulham move. Bill Glazier in goal had no chance. Clarke is wearing an unfamiliar number nine shirt instead of ten to accommodate new signing Joe Gilroy. This was Coventry's first-ever season in the First Division. Fulham won the match 3–0, and put together three league wins in a row, their best spell in a dismal season. At the end of the season Coventry survived by one point, but Fulham were relegated, six points adrift from safety.

Long before the Cravenettes and cheerleaders we had the Golden Girls who were after your money to provide much-needed funds for the club. Who could resist?

* * *

The Statmaster adds some detail: Here's a 3G lady from the early Seventies. Not modern 3G technology, but a Golden Goals Girl. The Golden Goals replaced the lucky number draw. Each ticket contained a minutes and seconds figure (eg 23 mins 12 seconds) and if this matched the time of the first goal, the prize of £25 was won. There was also £10 for the time of the second goal.

For the most part, I try to find pictures that show Fulham players in a good light. Not difficult, of course. But I fear I cannot talk my way round this photo. It really does look as though Tony Gale is behaving slightly less than immaculately in the 3–0 victory over Stoke in December 1977. Watching the action, which surely had to be a penalty, is Ray Evans.

*   *   *

Fulham's full back Evans, who scored that day, eventually left to join Stoke. The Stoke player in the picture is Garth Crooks, later to join Spurs. Crooks is now a TV pundit with the BBC and has filled out slightly since his lithe youthful days pictured here. The photo could well give Crooks plenty to talk about. Indeed, it might also give Tony Gale himself a lot to talk about, as he too is a respected television pundit. Is Gale's outstretched leg 'inviting the trip', or is Crooks deliberately running into the defender; anyway, whose arms are all over whom?

Sean O'Driscoll was one of those players who just got on with his football, quietly contributing quality and class to the team. Here he shows fine control at a near deserted Oxford in March 1981 – but couldn't prevent a 0–2 defeat for the Whites.

Opposite page: I do like this picture of Gerry Peyton captured in mid-air during our match against Bristol Rovers in April 1982. When I looked at it more closely, however, I noticed the legs in the background beneath Gerry, and rather wished they weren't in the picture. So I went into my computer and Photoshopped them out. That's the result on the right. I promise this was only done for a bit of fun. Neither Ashwater nor I would ever do such manipulation for real. Honest.

One of our favourite players and a typical picture of him. It's Roger Brown getting in the thick of things against Bristol Rovers in April 1982. This effort wasn't a goal, but he did get one in the game, which we won 4–2 on the way to promotion from Division Three.

* * *

The unstoppable force Brown played in every league match that season, netting twelve goals. Thirty years on, those twelve goals remain a record for a player in the 'centre back' position, though Kit Symons (see opposite) ran him very close almost twenty years later.

Kit Symons gets in a flying header at former club Manchester City in January 1999. A packed house of over 30,000 saw Fulham lose 0–3, but that was the only defeat during a run of twenty-one matches, and by the end of the season we were Division Two champions by a margin of fourteen points. Who could have imagined that some fifteen years later Symons would become caretaker manager of Fulham?

*   *   *   **

Kit Symons missed only one league game that season and ended up with eleven league goals from a centre half position (see caption opposite). The season produced no fewer than twenty-two different goalscorers, with Kit finishing as the second highest. Fulham conceded just thirty-two goals in the forty-six league games – what would we give for those stats today!

Sometimes a goal makes a rather static picture, but I always feel the moment is worth recording, as with this goal by Kit Symons (in yellow) in the 1–1 draw at Bournemouth in March 1999. This is one of the eleven league goals he scored that season, as mentioned on page 49.

Opposite: This is Ernie Howe, a classy defender who played for us between 1973 and 1977. I believe his refrain went, 'Six foot two, eyes of blue, Ernie Howe is after you.'

*   *   *

Like Sean O'Driscoll and Gordon Davies, Ernie was a bargain buy from the lower leagues, plucked from the Denbigh Road side, Hounslow Town, in 1973. Ernie weighed in with a fair few goals too for a centre half, netting seven in one season, including six in a three-month spell. He had a penchant for scoring in front of the cameras, including two in the 4–0 win over West Bromwich Albion featured on Match Of The Day in August 1975, when the programme decided to cover a second division match. He also scored when The Big Match covered Fulham's 2–0 victory over Chelsea a month later. Mind you, he was also captured on camera scoring a textbook own goal, when he neatly nodded past Fulham keeper Peter Mellor in the 4–1 victory over Hereford in September 1976. Ernie later played for QPR and Portsmouth and had considerable success as manager of non-league Basingstoke over a period of 13 years.

I continue to be delighted with what a computer can do to old slides. This picture, taken on transparency film, has languished in my files for nearly fifty years, neglected because of its poor colour and poor contrast. However, modern scanning has removed all marks and scratches, and a picture editing programme has restored colour and brightness. The result is this picture of our match at Coventry in November 1967 showing Steve Earle shooting on goal, with Jimmy Conway and Johnny Haynes in the background.

The Statmaster enjoys this view of a 'proper' Sixties stadium (Highfield Road) with its lack of concrete and multi-tier seating! You can almost sense the atmosphere, he says as his eyes mist over. Even so he has to add that the Coventry player in the picture is Northern Ireland international Dave Clements.

I find it hard to resist a good celebration picture like this! Here significant embracing is breaking out as Chris Coleman gets to grips with Kit Symons who has just scored one of our goals in the 3–1 victory over Reading in February 1999. Also entering the fray are Geoff Horsfield and Neil Smith.

What a privileged view I had when I went on to the Cottage balcony! Here I snapped the overall scene during the match against Southampton in April 1978. It's a memory of crowded terraces and a riverside stand that over 35 years later is due for re-development.

*   *   *

We managed a creditable 1–1 draw with a goal from centre half John Lacy. It was Lacy's last goal for the club and he moved to Division One Spurs at the end of the season for £200,000, one of the first fees to be decided by tribunal. Saints finished as runners-up and were promoted to the First Division. We finished very much mid-table, having scored 49 goals and conceded 49 goals.

Don't be fooled – we're playing in red here! This is a rare colour picture from me of us playing at Tottenham, in September 1977. I'm not too happy with it as I can't find the ball anywhere in the picture! The Fulham players are, from left, Ray Evans, Terry Bullivant and Peter Storey. And there's another reason I'm not too happy with it – Peter Storey. The late Dennis Turner, he of Fulham history and statistics, had no love for Storey because of his actions both on and off the field. Whenever Dennis had to compile a list of statistics that would include Storey, he would if at all possible contrive to stop the list before it got to that player's name. Nice one, Dennis.

* * *

This was Spurs' only season outside the top flight in recent years, a place they regained at the end of the season by finishing third. Our two matches against them were very close – the unlucky 0–1 defeat featured here at White Hart Lane, and an entertaining rain-soaked 1–1 televised draw at Craven Cottage, secured by a late Brian Greenaway goal. The two Spurs players in the foreground of the picture are John Pratt and Peter Taylor. Taylor won four England caps as a third division player with Crystal Palace, and has coached and managed England teams at various levels.

He never played for the club, but here is David Lloyd, a real Fulham legend who has produced TOOFIF, the famed Fulham fanzine, for over twenty-five years – what a magnificent achievement! He's pictured selling an issue chronicling the 2013–14 season. Unfortunately the light has caught the glossy covers of the magazines, but David's summing up of the season – 'Omnishambles' – is just about visible.

Action from striker Alan Warboys during the match against Blackburn in September 1977. Looking on are John Mitchell and, in the background, Les Strong.

*   *   *

The much travelled Warboys was rather unlucky in his brief stay at Fulham. He was often starved of service in a declining team. This match – a drab goalless home draw – typified that! This was Warboys' final Fulham game, and a week later he moved to Hull City.

This is the first Fulham match that I took my camera to. It's rather fitting that the opponents in this reserve match in September 1960 were Brentford, for, as our club slipped out of the Premiership in 2014, we were due to meet promoted Brentford in season 2014–15. (Actually, I don't think we slipped out of the top tier, I reckon we plummeted.) My picture is a good reminder of the cranes of the timber yard behind the Hammersmith End terracing. In those day our properly constituted reserve team played in a competition named the Football Combination; we were in the second division.

    Apologies for any tiny white dust marks that may be visible on the picture. It would have taken me ages to remove them all, so I made the executive decision to keep them in, reckoning they add a vintage quality to the photograph.

*   *   *

For the record, Fulham won this match 5–2. Goals from Mike Johnson, Allan Jones and Tosh Chamberlain gave Fulham a three-goal half-time advantage, but Brentford pulled the score back to 3–2. However, a further goal from Jones and one from Jimmy Hill secured the win. For Hill it was a goal against his former club in his final season as a player. He was playing for the reserve side working his way back from injury.

    Next season (2014–15), it will be almost 70 years since Fulham last met the Bees in the second tier of English football.

At the time of writing this was our last match in the Premiership – May 11th 2014. I took the picture in the last minute of added time and managed to capture our equalising goal in the 2–2 draw at home to Crystal Palace. The goal was scored by Chris David (number 30) with a fine curling shot inside the far post. Our other goal that day was scored by Cauley Woodrow (number 25). Two cracking goals from two fine youngsters; there's hope for the future! The other Fulham players in the picture are Hugo Rodallega and Steve Sidwell.

Sean Davis is pictured here at the very beginning of his career that saw him progress from the youth team into the first team. He scored memorable promotion-winning goals at Blackburn and Sheffield Wednesday in season 2000–01 and has the distinction of playing in all four divisions for the club.

This is Adrian Cambriani, a superb flying winger from our first rugby league days. I pictured him here at York, one of many new venues I was delighted to visit during the two seasons when the game was played at the Cottage.

In May 2010 our star defender Roger Brown came to the Cottage for an evening of camaraderie which had been arranged to help Roger who was suffering from cancer. I was proud to be part of the gathering, and this is one of my pictures that evening. It shows another former star, player and manager Malcolm Macdonald, chatting to one of the club's famed backroom staff, Gerry Kertons, who was kitman for many years. Also in the picture is one of our favourite ladies, Sandra Coles of the ticket office. Sandra has now retired after many years of sterling service with the club.

And here is a team group I managed to get during the Roger Brown evening in May 2010. I cannot imagine what I said to get them all smiling... Standing from left are: Les Strong, Bobby Campbell, Malcolm Macdonald, Ray Lewington, Dean Coney, Brian Greenaway, Steve Hatter, Ray Houghton, Dale Tempest, Roger Brown, Tony Gale, Derry Quigley, Jimmy Richardson, John Griffen, Gordon Davies, Robert Wilson and Terry Mancini. In front are Gerry Peyton, Gerry Kertons and Sean O'Driscoll.

It was a great gathering for a great colleague. Sadly, Roger succumbed to his illness and died in August 2011.

NEXT
HOME
GAME

BARCLAYS PREMIER LEAGUE

Sunday   11 May K.O. 15:00

Crystal Palace

The end of an era. This is May 2014 and our last match of the season. We are already relegated from the Premiership, and an unhappy season is coming to an end. What might the Maestro be thinking?

Actually Haynes had seen it all in his career – relegation as well as success. He stood by the club to become our greatest ever player.

This was taken on Kevin Keegan's last day as manager of Fulham before he went to take over the England manager's job. Kevin was always friendly and approachable and we fans enjoyed his time with us. Here he poses with my late friend and colleague Alan Williams, one of those supporters who worked tirelessly for the club behind the scenes and was a major figure in the Fulham 2000 campaign that fought to save the club during the dark days when it seemed it might go out of existence. He was also a great supporter of the Ashwater cause, and his friendship and enthusiasm are much missed.

A group of hard-working maintenance men photographed in the Enclosure in the Seventies.

A group of proud Fulham fans photographed at Blackpool in the Seventies. The intrepid 'Traveller' – Ashwater author the late, much missed Alex Ferguson – appears towards the left of the picture, wearing the diagonally striped scarf. Keeping up his spectacular attendance record, he's part of a happy group of supporters standing safely and even drinking an occasional can of beer. There don't seem to be too many health and safety issues.

Roy Bentley played for us with distinction from 1956 to 1961. He also had a minor success when he managed another west London club to their first league championship – that was Chelsea in 1955. In May 2004 he celebrated his 80th birthday and a group of friends gathered to honour him. Here is my picture taken on that occasion; since I'm in it you may contend that it's not actually one of my pictures! Well, I did put the camera on a tripod and I did set the self-timer and I did run back to get in the picture, so I'm claiming it as mine.

In the front are David Hamilton, Jimmy Hill, Roy the birthday boy, Roy's wife Vi, George Cohen and yours truly. What illustrious company for me!

*   *   *

Bentley's class and experience, especially once he had switched from the forward line to defence, were key in getting Fulham back to the First Division in 1959. So good was he that many were calling for him to be restored to the national team. The England manager agreed, but there was one sticking point – Roy was already 36!

Action from our 1–0 victory at Millwall in October 1998, as Paul Peschisolido is thwarted by a spirited defender. The photographer in the background is using a camera with a large telephoto lens, though it looks as though he may be watching the action rather than watching the viewfinder. However, I have to report that he hasn't missed much in his career since then, for this is Javier Garcia, one of the greats of sports photography. He has his own sports photography company, is a thoroughly nice chap – and a good friend of Ashwater.

Barry Hayles, on the edge of the penalty area, scores the only goal of the FA Cup third-round replay against Wycombe Wanderers in January 2002. Three defenders couldn't stop him. We supporters could have told them that.

*   *   *

This goal finally dented the hopes of the Chairboys, after a 2–2 draw at Adams Park. The replay was a tense and bruising encounter with significant physical excess.

    Wycombe were managed at the time by Lawrie Sanchez, later to put his style on Fulham as manager in 2007. Fulham were lucky to have escaped with a replay in the first match, only a late goal by Steve Marlet having saved them from defeat against the team two divisions below them. However, from this inauspicious start Fulham progressed to an FA Cup semi-final, their first in twenty-seven years.

Steve Finnan crashes in a shot against Millwall in April 1999. What a cultured player he was! Also in the picture are Kevin Betsy, a young player who promised much but didn't quite deliver, and Paul Peschisolido.

*   *   *

Betsy, signed from Woking for £80,000, was unlucky to be bought alongside more illustrious players. He managed just one goal for Fulham – in this match. The match was yet another five-star show from the Cottagers, full of flamboyant attacking football, and the 4–1 scoreline was the least they deserved.

On our way to promotion in season 1998–99, we went to Reading's new stadium in April and won by this goal from Simon Morgan. Simon looks suspiciously offside in my picture, though that can be deceptive. However, he even looks suspiciously offside in the television pictures of the match.

The aftermath of the goal opposite, but a little too early for the scoreboard.

Before the era of selfies, Geoff Horsfield reaches up to sign a fan's programme, and duly returns the biro.

Our former chairman Mohamed Al Fayed enjoyed his regular pre-match amble around the pitch. Here he stops to do a Horsfield.

A nineteenth-century photographer, Eadweard Muybridge, was challenged to determine whether a galloping horse ever has all four legs off the ground. He set up a number of cameras fired by trip wires and proved that, yes, at some moments the horse is completely off the ground. Well, that's rather a long-winded way of identifying one reason why I like this picture, as all four feet of these two players are off the ground. The Fulham player is John Evanson, pictured here flying at the Blackburn defence in December 1976. In the background is Les Strong (how does he get in so many of my pictures?) but he has his feet pretty firmly on the ground.

*　　*　　*

On a bitterly cold and icy evening, under 9,000 saw Fulham record a much needed 2–0 victory. The win was one of just three victories in a sequence of twenty-six league and cup matches, of which fifteen were lost. However five wins in the last eleven league matches saw the Whites achieve a safe seventeenth place in the Division Two table.

Oh no, not another picture of the Cravenettes dancing on the pitch. Actually that's not why I've included it. This was a view (rather restricted!) from a corner of Loftus Road during our stay there from 2002 to 2004, and what I like is the banner in the picture – a sunrise badge and the message 'Cookie's Black and White Army'.

I have to say that the badge doesn't look any better back to front. Having been brought up with traditional badges, of which Fulham's was a classic example (have a look at page 60), I find the current one uninspired. Fans sometimes argue with me that the badge is actually good, as it is very recognisable. That may be true but it's not the point. A black circle would be just as recognisable, but it would offer nothing about our club and our history. We are proud of being 'London's Original'; surely we should celebrate that with style.

Steed Malbranque acclaims a goal in our 2–0 win over Leicester in October 2003. Both goals that day were scored by Luis Boa Morte. For his goal pictured here, Luis shot from the edge of the goal area, beating the goalkeeper all ends up.

* * *

The goalkeeper here is Ian Walker. The game was part of a heady run of just two defeats in the first ten games of the 2003–04 season, under Chris Coleman's stewardship. Fulham finished the season mid-table, but opponents Leicester were relegated after just one season back in the Premiership.

And this is the other goal in the match featured opposite. Boa Morte makes it look easy from just ten yards. With all the players looking at the goalkeeper I had to examine the picture closely to see where the ball was. It's actually just disappearing behind the goalie's thighs. A fraction of a second's delay in taking the photo might have produced a better picture. But better this picture than none at all.

A tussle involving our Geoff Horsfield at Reading in April 1999 – and a rare glimpse of Neil Smith. At the end of the season Smith joined Reading.

Here's a goal from our 2–0 victory at home to Aston Villa in October 1972. John Mitchell emphatically thumps the ball home from inside the goal area. The other goal that sunny afternoon was scored by Alan Mullery, watching this goal at left in the picture. The other Fulham player, number 7, is Les Strong (yes, him again!) who started his career on the right wing. He's just cut the ball back for Mitchell to score.

*   *   *

Mullery's goal came after just two minutes from a twice-taken free kick. Aston Villa arrived as league leaders, but were well beaten by an energetic performance.

Rodney Marsh preparing for action in the dressing room. This was during his second spell with us.

Teddy Maybank was a wonderful, fearless player and never held back when going in for the ball. Here he is caught in a flying tangle with a Rovers defender at Bristol in August 1977. The action was just too fast for me to focus correctly, which I regret, but I think it's better to have a picture like this than no picture at all.

There was plenty of endeavour from both sides in the match but, on a hot afternoon, neither team could manage a goal.

Maurice Cook tussles with an Aston Villa defender in March 1963. Johnny Key looks on.

* * *

The Villa defender is Charlie Aitken. Key made 181 appearances during his ten years at the club, scoring 37 goals. The match was won by a single goal, scored by debutant Rodney Marsh. It was his only appearance that season, and it took him another season to be established in the team.

Bit difficult to know what's going on here. I know it's against Millwall in December 1976, and I know it was a muddy, snow-covered pitch. But what Brian Greenaway and Barry Kitchener are up to is anyone's guess. And is it Brian's hand on the ball? Could be. But it might not be deliberate. Maybe it was ball to hand. And was it really a white ball on the snow?

*   *   *

Fulham lost this last game of the year 2–3. The young Greenaway was getting a rare game on the wing, replacing the injured George Best. The tussle was very much a 'Little and Large' affair, as the slightly built Greenaway was up against the massive frame of the Millwall giant.

Teddy Maybank volleys home one of his two goals in the 2–1 victory over Orient in the League Cup first-round second-leg match in August 1977. But this cracking goal wasn't enough to save Fulham as they had lost the first leg match 0–2. This first-round exit was followed later in the season by exit from the FA Cup at the first attempt (0–1 at Burnley), leaving the club to play out a mediocre season under manager Bobby Campbell.

*   *   *

The helpless Orient defenders are Bobby Fisher and Phil Hoadley. The goalkeeper is John Smeulders. Both legs of this tie were played at Craven Cottage because of essential drainage works still being carried out on the Orient pitch.

This photograph features one of a small group of players who played just one game for the club. The number 10 pictured here at Southampton in November 1977 is Colin McCurdy. He looks to have a good chance to score, but his effort went the wrong side of the post (picture below). He was subsequently substituted in the match – and that was the sum of his Fulham career.

* * *

Not only did McCurdy fail to score in the match, so did the team, and we lost 0–2. The unlucky McCurdy had been signed from Irish side Larne, but sustained an injury which kept him out of football for months. After one more season at Fulham, he tried his luck in the USA.

I suspect you won't believe me, but this suggests that photographers are human after all. George Best and Rodney Marsh had just signed for the club in August 1976, too late to play in the match at Charlton, and so watched the match from the dugout. A photographer colleague just couldn't resist the opportunity to get the autographs of the famous duo. I wonder if he's still got that programme.

I was wondering why I had gone into our dressing room at Millwall's old Den in December 1977, but the smiling faces of manager Bobby Campbell and coach Ken Craggs were the clue. We had just thumped the Lions 3–0, and a celebratory cup of tea had to be caught on camera.

We secured a thumping victory over Burnley at Craven Cottage in October 1977 by four goals to one. This is one of the two goals that John Mitchell scored that evening. The other goals came from Tony Mahoney and George Best. The Statmaster informs me that the well-beaten prostrate goalkeeper is Alan Stevenson.

Action from a sunny afternoon in September 1962 when a packed crowd of over 30,000 welcomed Everton to the Cottage. My picture shows George Cohen attempting to close down an Everton forward. The Fulham player watching the action is centre half Bill Dodgin, then nearing the end of his career. Some six years later he returned to the club as manager following the sacking of Bobby Robson.

*   *   *

Dodgin was in his second spell at Fulham, after a sojourn at Arsenal; just two months later he sustained a broken leg. Fulham won this match 1–0 without car crash victim Johnny Haynes. His replacement, a young Stan Brown, scored the goal, in only his second game for the club. The Everton players in the foreground of the picture are Alex Young and Roy Vernon. Our victory was one of just six defeats for the Toffees, who finished as league champions.

This is March 1963 and a visit from Blackpool on a muddy pitch, the like of which we never see today, and this was the second goal of our 2–0 victory. It was scored by Maurice Cook, not in the picture. The two Fulham players are Jackie Henderson (I think) and Graham Leggat.

*   *   *

The win was the third in a run of eight consecutive victories in the top flight, which included defeats of both the Manchester clubs. Fulham have never equalled such a winning sequence. At the rear of the picture is Jimmy Armfield, who was a rival to George Cohen for the England No 2 shirt. Armfield is now one of the best informed pundits on the radio.

Eddie Lowe played the last of over 500 games for the club in May 1963. The match was against Birmingham City and here he comes out to the pitch on his own whilst the rest of the team wait as he posed for the cameramen and took the warm applause of the crowd. It was a genuinely emotional moment.

In the centre of the picture just in front of the right-hand gate-post is a smiling Johnny Haynes, still struggling with injury following his car crash the previous August.

*   *   *

Defender Lowe's career at Fulham spanned thirteen years. This, his final match for the club, produced an entertaining 3–3 draw. It wasn't a great afternoon for defenders, though. Two of Fulham's goals were obligingly scored by Birmingham players Smith and Green.

Johnny Haynes was always a welcome visitor to the Cottage after he retired and went to play and live in South Africa. He returned in December 1975 for the second leg of the Anglo-Scottish Cup final against Middlesbrough and duly performed the half-time lucky numbers draw with Johnny Hartburn, here sporting a nifty Fulham tie. We lost the cup final by a single goal over the two legs – courtesy of an own goal by, ahem, Les Strong.

*   *   *

Johnny Hartburn was Fulham's 'Pools' promoter, a genial and smiling man who was always grateful to his agents for the few shillings raised each week. He had been a more than decent player too – a flying goal-scoring winger with Orient and QPR.

I can say with confidence that this picture has never been seen before. The negatives of this match, at Bury in March 1971, were immediately filed away, and have never seen the light of day until now. The match was a desultory 0–2 defeat in front of just over 4,000 spectators, and for my picture report of the match in Fulham's subsequent home programme, I had the effrontery to put in a blank space, with a comment that that was the best picture I got at the match... I don't think I'd get away with that now if I were working for the programme!

Nevertheless, it was a fair comment on an abysmal performance. Of the handful of pictures I managed to take of the match, this was the best. Fulham are playing in stripes and that's defender Dave Moreline at right attacking the Bury goal, trying to show Fulham's attack what they should be doing.

Somehow, it all came right in the end; in spite of this poor display we achieved promotion at the end of the season.

Two views of the riverside terracing. At the top, that's action against Arsenal in September 1962, with hardly a Fulham player in sight. It's a fond reminder of the wooden hut where half-time scores were posted up, as well as of the flags of all the clubs. Below that is a picture from the opening match of the 1971–72 season, against Watford; the terraces are being demolished in readiness for the new stand, but the flagpoles remain. I believe they're still there.

An FA Cup goal scored from distance by Louis Saha against Birmingham City in January 2003. We won the match 3–1. In the foreground of the picture is Facundo Sava, who also scored that day.

*   *   *

The match produced a final goal in Fulham colours for Bjarne Goldbaek (at top in the picture) during a rare appearance that season. Birmingham's number 8 is the infamous Robbie Savage, who is now a regular pundit on radio and TV. He can rarely resist putting his foot in it – referring to his punditry, of course, not his football.

In the midst of this crowd of journalists huddled near the Cottage entrance is a footballer just signed by Fulham in 1976. It is, of course, George Best, and I'm surprised that, as a mere photographer, I could get this close.

So, that's what a cup looks like... Fulham Ladies enjoy their triumph after beating Tottenham Ladies 4–1 in the League Cup final in April 1999.

An embrace from Barry Hayles as he tussles for the ball with a Wrexham defender in April 1999.

*   *   *

The Whites were already promoted at this stage, and were a little stale following an exhilarating 4–1 victory over Millwall in midweek. Against Wrexham on the Saturday they managed a 1–1 draw thanks to a Paul Peschisolido goal.

In the shadow of the Torquay stand, Fulham suffer a 1–2 defeat in February 1996, and slip to next to bottom of the Football League, peering into the Football Conference. It was the lowest spot in the club's history. In the picture Mike Conroy (scorer on the day) is for once outjumped by defenders whilst Nick Cusack and Rory Hamill look on.

A perfect penalty – and a perfect penalty picture. Well, I think so, anyway! Alan Mullery scores our goal in the 1–1 draw at Notts County in August 1974.

We secured a 1–0 victory at home to Oldham in January 1999, and this was the goal that did it. Finding himself clear in the penalty area, Simon Morgan slams in an unstoppable shot that comprehensively beats the goalkeeper.

*   *   *

This was a freezing night and there was a late finish to the match, due to the late arrival of the Oldham team coach that had found itself stuck in traffic.

Physio Ron Woolnough applies high-tech treatment to injured goalkeeper Peter Mellor – the magic spray. At least it was one step up from the magic sponge. Bobby Moore and Les Strong look on with that expression which says, 'Come on, mate. Get on with it.'

*   *   *

Johnny Haynes was noted for it – there seems to be a lot of 'hands on hipping' from the players! Oh, and does that spell 'OUCH' on Woolnough's track suit? The match was the famous 4–1 defeat of Hereford at Craven Cottage in September 1976.

Fulham had a good run in the FA Cup in 1999. Whilst still a Division Two (third tier) team, they went to Premiership pace-setters Aston Villa in the fourth round and achieved a comprehensive 2–0 victory. This is the first goal, scored early on. It came from a corner fired in by Steve Hayward (at far left in the picture) and was a superb flashing header by Simon Morgan (not in the picture). Paul Peschisolido is already celebrating.

*   *   *

The Statmaster points out that the player unable to keep the ball out by the near post is 17-year-old Gareth Barry in his debut season. Fulham were unluckily edged out in the next round 0–1 at Old Trafford.

We had a good season in 1970–71, finally achieving promotion from the old Division Three. Our visit to Halifax in March 1971 saw us record one of our few defeats, and we lost 1–2 to the Shaymen on a muddy pitch via two late goals. This was our goal, bundled in by George Johnston in the first half. It came from a run and centre from Jimmy Conway (at left).

This was one of the few football grounds where it was perfectly acceptable for photographers to stand up near the goal rather than sit, and I do recall doing that.

And here's George Johnston again, in action against Shrewsbury Town just a few weeks after the Halifax match opposite. This time it's sunshine, a flying defender, but no goals in the match.

*   *   *

This was a rather jaded performance, but we won the final two tough away games – at Doncaster and Bradford City   to secure promotion back to Division Two. What would today's pundits have to say about the height of the defender's flying foot?

A hot day at Millwall in August 1968, and a determined John Dempsey in vivid away colours in the shadow of the stand.

*   *   *

Dempsey was an under-rated defender who came through the ranks. He starred in the great escape of 1965–66 and became a mainstay of the defence. Although London born, he qualified to play for Eire, and won seven caps whilst at Fulham. He had a spell for Fulham at centre forward where he scored five goals in three games, including a hat-trick against Northampton in the League Cup. He moved across to Chelsea in late 1968 as the main part of the deal which brought Barry Lloyd to Fulham.

The fondly-remembered Bobby Keetch fires in a shot on the Burnley goal in December 1964. It was to no avail, as Fulham lost the match 0–1. The other Fulham players are Bobby Howfield and Rodney Marsh.

*   *   *

Perhaps Keetch was already getting frustrated. Not only did Fulham lose, but it was his mix-up with goalkeeper Tony Macedo that presented Burnley with their winning goal. Later in the match Keetch was sent off following an altercation with Burnley scorer Willie Irvine.

For some reason that I cannot recall, I didn't file my colour slide pictures as assiduously as I did my Fulham negatives. Consequently I have no record of when this picture was taken. Though it must have been around 1967 to 1968, as it features our Scottish forward Joe Gilroy.

*   *   *

It's actually April 1968 and Gilroy sidefoots another effort on the Newcastle goal as defender Frank Clark takes evasive action. On this occasion, unlike the previous season, Newcastle had remembered to bring their change strip! Fulham won this match comfortably 2–0 with two goals from Allan Clarke (here pictured on the floor). A victory at Bramall Lane three days later brought hope of a relegation escape. However, the next two matches were lost, and that spelled the end of nine years at the top for the Cottagers.

Now, that's how to capture the ball going into the net! This was one of our goals in the 3–1 defeat of Reading in February 1999. It's probably one of the two goals that Geoff Horsfield scored that evening. But where's the goalscorer? Not in the picture, I fear. The Fulham players who do appear in the photo are Kit Symons and Barry Hayles.

The year 2014 was the 50th anniversary of BBC's Match of the Day programme. This picture was almost certainly taken in the very early days when the programme was broadcast briefly on BBC2. The photograph, never seen before, shows Steve Earle flashing in a shot at the Hammersmith end. Once again it's over to the Statmaster for the facts. I can tell him it was a rainy day with little wind.

* * *

The match is against Sheffield Wednesday in April 1966, and this is almost certainly the goal that Steve Earle scored that day. The game was part of that season's original 'Great Escape', and Fulham came from behind twice to beat the Owls 4–2. The other goals were scored by Bobby Robson with a penalty, Les Barrett and Graham Leggat.

Opposite: Manager Alec Stock welcomes new signings Paul Went and John Cutbush to the Cottage in 1972. I clearly wasn't the only photographer present on this occasion. but I regret I cannot remember whether the snapper in my picture was a lady or a gentleman – and I still can't be sure from the picture. Ah, those were the days.

* * *

Stock had just been installed as manager, and had made a flagship signing with the acquisition of Alan Mullery. Went and Cutbush were two other significant signings, at opposite ends of the fee scale – Went cost a club record £80,000 from Charlton, whilst Cutbush was a free acquisition from Spurs. Both performed admirably and Cutbush went on to play for the Whites in the FA Cup final in 1975. Went's stay at the Cottage was brief, and just fifteen months later he was sold to Division Two rivals Portsmouth for a club record £155,000. He was sold (along with Steve Earle to Leicester for £100,000) in order to pay off a huge chunk of the debt still remaining on the new riverside stand. This wasn't the only time that supporters were informed that money had been brought in to help pay off the stand, though its original cost had only been about £250,000.

In December 1981, whilst in Division Three, we lost 0–1 at first division Tottenham in the fourth round of the League Cup. This picture is of the elegant and powerful Dean Coney in full flight during the match.

* * *

The match saw us bow out of the competition to an early Micky Hazard goal, but we outplayed Spurs for long periods in the second half and were unlucky not to equalise on a number of occasions. It was the north London side who were much relieved to hear the final whistle.

Opposite: This picture is from our FA Cup run of the 1981–82 season. We went to Bristol Rovers in November and two Dean Coney goals saw us through, but we somehow lost in the next round to Hereford United. My picture shows much delight from Fulham players Coney, Gordon Davies, Robert Wilson and current England coach Ray Lewington, whilst the Rovers keeper forlornly retrieves the ball from his goal.

Before David Hamilton, there was another cultured voice broadcasting to the fans. He was Don Durbridge, a much respected broadcaster, who played records from his kiosk on the Cottage balcony, and kept us all informed. Commercial director and former player Jimmy Hill gets in the picture.

It's getting towards the end of this book, and it's hard work writing all the captions. Oh, yes, it is! So how about you writing your own caption here. It's a moment from a match during the demolition of the riverside terraces.

Captions referring to policemen's balls will be frowned upon.

The Thamesbank Travellers were a renowned, even notorious, group of fans who magically found their way to all Fulham's away matches. Here they were guests at a Fulham function in the Riverside suite in the Seventies, and, to nobody's surprise, they had brought their flag with them. The banner appears to have been signed by the Fulham players, who I'm sure appreciated the Travellers' support. At left in the picture are Alan Mullery and two ladies looking on in awe.

An offbeat picture of the Cottage balcony railings. A similar shot was used for the cover of the official Fulham programme for the match against Sunderland in October 1973. I'm still not sure whether it really was a suitable cover picture.

This may not be one of my most exciting pictures, but it is a rare glimpse of Fulham playing on foreign soil. Well, Scotland, to be precise. This was one of our Anglo-Scottish Cup forays, visiting Heart of Midlothian in October 1975. We drew this second-leg quarter-final match 2–2 with goals from Alan Slough and Alan Mullery, winning the tie 5–4 on aggregate. Here the masterful Bobby Moore (at right) marshals the Fulham defence and clears an attack. The other Fulham players are Scotsman John Dowie, Alan Slough, Ernie Howe and Alan Mullery.

I'd forgotten that we had Fulham cheergirls as long ago as 1982. Here they make their presence felt at the match against Bristol Rovers in April, though the fans do seem distinctly unimpressed.

*   *   *

A delightful picture of young ladies shaking their maracas.

Barry Lloyd takes a summer break from football and smashes a four during a cricket match on Putney Common in the Seventies.

* * *

This was an annual event with the Putney Cricket Club, a traditional curtain-raiser to the football season. Don't be fooled, the Cottagers had a number of first-class cricketers, and most of the first team, coaches and medical staff took part. Would it have been possible to hear the cry 'Earle's caught!'?

The man in the middle here is referee Roger Kirkpatrick, often called Mr Pickwick because of his Edwardian sideburns and his portly bearing, and renowned for sudden bursts of running backwards during a match. He delighted in drawing attention to himself, seeming to think he was the star of the show. Fans sometimes described him in different terms. Here it looks as though he is injured and subsequent pictures that I took suggest he went off injured, though I cannot remember the match or the incident, and the piece of film with those pictures on is filed separately from any match.

*   *   *

This happened during the 1–1 draw at home to Bristol City in October 1974. Mr Kirkpatrick couldn't continue and was replaced by a linesman. In the picture Jimmy Conway watches developments whilst City skipper Geoff Merrick (at rear) takes the opportunity to reorganise his troops.

Elsewhere in these captions I mention that Teddy Maybank was not fearful of getting in where it hurt – and that's him at right getting to grips with former club Chelsea during our 1–2 defeat at the Cottage in March 1980. What I didn't expect to see is our Gordon Davies (number 9) getting in where any man would fear to go – up against Micky Droy. No wonder we called Gordon our Welsh terrier.

* * *

This was a tough old match, and Roger Brown's debut lasted less than one half. In the melee pictured, Chopper Harris is as usual involved, and referee Ken Baker attempts to separate Maybank from Butch Wilkins' brother Graham. Fulham were undone that day by two goals from Clive Walker – who would join Fulham seven years later.

Just a favourite goal picture – a superb header from Steve Earle against Newcastle in the 5–1 victory in February 1967. Allan Clarke watches in admiration.

A happy picture of a lovely man. This is Alec Stock, our manager from 1972 to 1976, who took us – and me, in the team coach! – to Wembley.

* * *

Apart from one mediocre season with Roma, Stock knew nothing but success as a manager, be it at Yeovil, Leyton Orient, Queen's Park Rangers, Luton and, of course, Fulham. Never a tracksuit manager, he's here pictured impeccably dressed as ever, with collar and tie and pocket handkerchief.

Renowned goal-poacher Gordon Davies scored a hat-trick at Leicester in September 1979. Here's one of the goals. Peter Kitchen looks on admiringly.

* * *

The well beaten Leicester keeper is Mark Wallington. This was Gordon's second hat-trick in seven league games. Despite Davies' three, Leicester also managed three in what was a full-blooded encounter. However, equality between the teams had vanished by the end of the season as the Foxes finished as Division Two champions whilst the Whites were relegated.

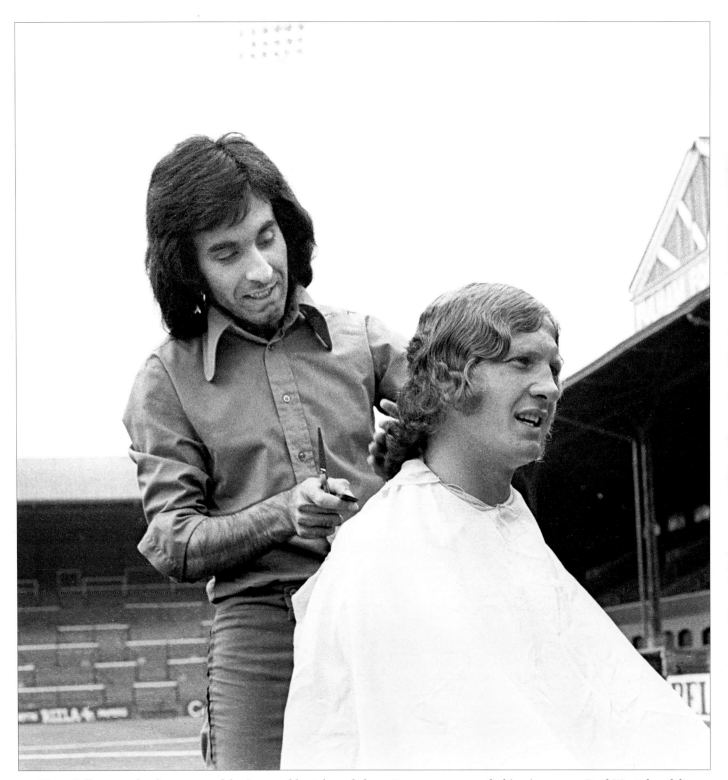

We at Fulham used to be renowned for impeccable style and class. Among our many fashion icons was Paul Went, he of the beautiful Seventies curls. Here he submits to a master snapper – the hairdresser, not me – or am I confusing my snippers with my snappers?

*   *   *

Manager Alec Stock was a former Army man, who wanted his players married, settled and behaving and looking 'like men'. He had little time for long hair, and decided to implement that on his arrival at the Cottage. In truth it caused a near mutiny amongst a few players, but the manager got his way. He always said, 'Pele didn't have to have long hair to be a great player'!

Here's a goal from Nick Cusack (centre of the picture) in our 2–0 victory at Doncaster in February 1996. His header beats despairing defenders, but Micky Conroy is on hand just in case. There is a slight lack of sharpness across the picture, which always upsets me. I try to console myself with the fact that the Doncaster floodlights were not too bright and I was pushing both film and camera to limits. More likely I got a bit excited at the prospect of a Fulham victory and my hand shook ever so slightly. I still like the picture, though!

A social event at Wimbledon dog track, where a number of Fulham personalities mingled happily with fans. Pictured here during a questions session from supporters are Nick Cusack, Terry Angus and Alan Cork.

Season 1965–66 saw our first great escape when, after being down and out in February, we won nine of our next eleven matches to escape relegation by two points. By the time we played our last home game, against Stoke, we needed one point for safety. We duly drew the match 1–1, with Allan Clarke's first goal for the club. Here Steve Earle bursts into the Stoke penalty area for another attack.

A 5–0 defeat of Watford on a freezing Boxing Day in 2000 was one of many highlights of a wonderful season that saw us promoted into the Premiership. Two of our goals that day are pictured on these pages. Here Barry Hayles plants the ball past a floundering goalkeeper. It was one of three goals Hayles scored that day.

Here's another of the five goals we scored against Watford in December 2000. Andres Stolcers turns away after planting the ball past a floundering goalkeeper.

*   *   *

At the time this was billed as a 'winner takes all' match, as Watford were flying high alongside the Cottagers. The game was much hyped. But come the day there was only one team in it, and it signified a downturn in Watford's fortunes as they finished a disappointing ninth. Fulham ended up as champions by ten clear points.

The refrain still goes, 'Who put the ball in the Carlisle net', and the answer is Rodney McAree. Here he is doing it – at Brunton Park in April 1997, a key moment in our promotion season. I've always regretted that in the picture Matty Lawrence's arm (number 2) has just obscured McAree's face, but that's the way it goes. No problem with the ball, though. I managed to capture it in full flight on the way to the back of the net. The goal gave us a famous 2–1 victory, secured by two goals after trailing at half-time. For the record, our first goal was scored by Micky Conroy.

As the last light of a December afternoon fades away, five Fulham players celebrate one of our goals in the 3–1 victory over Tranmere Rovers In December 2000.

A gloomy afternoon at the Cottage, a churned-up muddy pitch, but John Marshall keeps his eye on the ball during the 2–1 victory over Exeter City in February 1996.

*   *   *

John was a versatile utility player who in twelve years from 1982 played nearly 500 games for the Whites. This was his final season as a player and, like Stan Brown before him, he played in every outfield position for the club – including substitute.

'Please help, gentlemen,' I said, 'I've been asked to photograph a van. Would you please gather round.' Taking a break from training before the 1996–97 season, they kindly obliged. They are (at rear) Paul Watson, Mike Conroy, Simon Stewart, Simon Morgan and Rob Scott (crouching), and at the front Darren Freeman, Glenn Cockerill, Tony Lange and Nick Cusack.

A memory of Craven Cottage from what seems like a bygone era. Veteran Bobby Robson is up with the attack in the televised 3–1 win over Sunderland in April 1967. Robson missed just one match in this his final season, as did Allan Clarke. John Dempsey went one better, not missing a single game.

*   *   *

This was one of only two victories between New Year and the end of the season. Our goals that day were scored by Allan Clarke, Steve Earle and Mark Pearson. Earle's goal was scored when coming on as a substitute, a feat he had also achieved just four days previously in the 1–2 defeat at Manchester United. Fulham played forty-eight matches that season, and eight first-teamers played forty or more games. The club's main thirteen players virtually picked themselves – what a difference to our chaotic season of 2013–14, where we used a record 43 players! Despite finishing that 1966–67 season in a lowly eighteenth place, the Fulham squad boasted ten international players: Macedo, McClelland, Cohen, Dempsey, Robson, Conway, Haynes, Clarke, Barrett and Leggat.

Celebration from the team following promotion in 1997, masterminded by manager Micky Adams (at left).

* * *

This was the first promotion for fifteen years and the first sign that the Fulham ship (as seen on the club's badge...) was slowly but surely being turned around. On a shoestring budget of youth, veterans, bargain buys and free transfers, Adams and Alan Cork (at right in the picture) moulded a team spirit and instilled a hunger that drove the players on to success.

Geoff Horsfield prods home a goal in the 2–2 draw against Luton Town in the third-round FA Cup tie in December 1999.

* * *

This was a real topsy-turvy cup run, very Fulhamish. In the 100th season of the Football League, we struggled against lower-level opposition Luton Town in this match, before winning the replay comprehensively 3–0. We then took on and beat Premiership side Wimbledon just as easily by the same score. Naturally this fuelled hopes of a meaningful cup run, so it was no surprise when three weeks later we drifted out of the competition in a 1–2 defeat at home to a mediocre Tranmere Rovers side, whom we'd beaten in the league just three weeks previously.

A determined defender shields the ball from Fulham's equally determined Vic Halom. Fred Callaghan looks on.

*   *   *

This was the Division Three championship decider in May 1971. Fulham were already promoted, and Preston looked likely to accompany them. Preston needed to win against what was a drained and lethargic Whites side. They had that extra bit of steel and determination to nick the match 0–1, with Fulham just unable to raise their game on the day. Preston won their last match a few days later to snatch the title, leaving the Cottagers as bridesmaids. In the picture the scorer of the Preston goal that day, Ricky Heppolette, is facing the camera between Callaghan and Halom.

A heart-warming picture from Roger Brown's celebratory evening in May 2010, and a memory of our lion-hearted defender. On Roger's right is Les Strong, and on his left are Robert Wilson and Gordon Davies.

A sunny walk through Bishop's Park on the way to a match at the Cottage. At the time of writing (summer 2014) the sun seems to have forsaken our favourite club, but I'm sure it will shine brightly again.